Jezebel, Her Unveiling

written by Rev. Wyatt Haws

Trafford rev. 01/29/2019

North America & international
toll-free: 1 888 232 4444 (USA & Canada)
fax: 812 355 4082

Our mission is to bring the revelation of Jesus Christ to the world and to heal families and the family of God of the evil plans which were made to steal, kill, and destroy it.

Light of the Fire Ministries

Table of Contents

IN THE FAMILY

The family is the basic unit of organization that we know of. In the family today there is dysfunction that is escalating to epidemic proportions.

This dysfunction is nothing new. There has been dysfunction in the family dating back to the Garden of Eden and continuing throughout history. The destruction of the family unit and all those within it is greater than ever in this generation.

In this document, we will discuss the reasons behind this explosion of destruction and shed light on the solution and the prophetic reason for it in this time frame.

To understand the problem we must first go and see what history can reveal to us about it. In the beginning, Eve was tempted by the serpent to eat of the tree of the knowledge of good and evil, the tree that God had told her and Adam **not** to eat from.

In her weakness, Eve fell victim to the serpent in eating from this forbidden tree. The serpent didn't stop there, he then tempted her to take the fruit to Adam and give it to him to eat also. In Adam's weakness, he fell to the temptation also and disobeyed God's orders. He failed to use his authority over the schemes of the serpent and from then on we have all been subject to sin and Satan's schemes.

The Bible gives many examples of this kind of destructive plan at work, some of which we will cover. For now let us give this plan the name that the Bible would reference it as, *the spirit of Jezebel*.

Jezebel was the wife of King Ahab. Ahab followed the ways of Adam and failed to take control of a very destructive scheme that led to Naboth's death.

In the same way, many men are doing the same thing today and the destructive forces of Jezebel's spirit are manifesting unimpeded. This is why the divorce rate is soaring, spousal abuse is rampant, children are rebelling and are being abused, and the family unit is being destroyed.

God had a better plan for the family unit. He gave the order of responsibility as such:
- the man or husband is to be the head,
- the woman is to be submissive to the husband,
- and the children were to obey and honor mother and father.

It is the same order that He has for His church:
- Jesus Christ,

- the church,
- and the children of God the Father.

The people are the church and people make up families so you can see why Satan would target the family unit for his schemes of stealing and killing and destroying. If he can destroy the families he then can destroy the bride of Christ, thus usurping the position of Jesus Christ, his plan from the beginning.

As we understand the plan we then can gather wisdom to overcome and walk in the victory that God would have for us to prosper in.

First the man must understand what is expected of him. God wants to have a relationship with him. In this relationship, man must take the *symbolic* form of being the female, otherwise we would have an abomination of homosexuality set up and the Bible tells us that Jesus Christ is the bridegroom.

In this relationship man is expected to obey or be submissive to following the Lord's commands. He is to build a relationship with God on trust and faith as that of a child. When this faith matures it will be accounted to the man as righteousness and in this righteousness man will be able to see Jesus Christ. When the man is able to see Him he then can believe in Him, asking the Father anything in His name and it will be given to him.

As this relationship grows, the man will begin to understand that his obedience will bring blessings and the abundance for himself and his family. He will also realize further what the Father expects from him and what he needs from the Father.

Galatians 5:22-23 lists the fruits of the Spirit. They are love, joy, peace, patience, kindness, goodness, faithfulness, gentleness, and self-control.

These are the attributes that men will want and desire from the Father and these are the attributes that the woman will want in a man. Because as this relationship transcends into the pattern for the husband and wife, the man will then take the position of the male and of course the woman the female. Every man can then understand what is needed and expected of him from his wife. It is the same things that he desires and needs from his relationship with the Father. The woman needs for her husband to exhibit the same fruits of the Spirit toward her, as he desires from the Father. And when this relationship is functioning properly, the children in the household will then have an example to follow in honoring mother and father and not being so rebellious.

The spirit of Jezebel is still at work trying to confuse and destroy this simple order. We live in a time where men are no longer men and women are no longer women. The plan is that we become a unisex society. That is Satan, who is the power of this world, trying to create a kingdom in the flesh which would be equal to the Kingdom of Jesus Christ in the spirit where there is not the distinction between male and female for we are all one in Christ.

Men need to be men and women need to be women again in order for victory to happen in our families.

What happens in the families where this division or dysfunction occurs, and it affects all families and all people, is the man fails to keep his relationship right with the Father. He allows the cares and stresses of the world to come between himself and the Father creating a breach in what needs to be a sound connection. It is something that happens but needs to be recognized and dealt with quickly. If not, the family order is distorted and an avenue for Jezebel to enter has occurred.

Soon there will be arguments instead of self-controlled reasoning. These arguments can lead to abusive situations where hitting and mental cruelty occur.

These are the responsibility of the man to stop, not throw his hands in the air and walk away from or worse, allow himself to beat his wife or children. A good deterrent for men to remember here is that by what ever measure you measure by is the measure by which you will be measured. If a man decides to abuse his wife by hitting her, he must realize that is the way he wants God to reprove him when he makes a mistake. Any man with any sense would not want to be in a hitting match with God. If he decides to throw his hands in the air and walk away he is deciding that he wants God to walk away when he is being tormented by an evil entity. By doing the latter, he is surrendering himself and his family over to the powers of Satan and not being submissive to God.

Instead he needs to recognize the need of his wife and come to a sound reasoning with her using the fruits of the Spirit. Just as God in Isaiah chapter one spoke to us to reason with Him in recognizing our transgression and sin and come into repentance and forgiveness, we must take the time to reason and come to an understanding of where the real enemy has infiltrated the family and defeat her or else she will devour everyone. In the book of Nahum chapter 3 verse 4 the Bible says, "All because of the many harlotries of the harlot, the charming one, the mistress of sorceries, who sells nations by her harlotries and families by her sorceries."

The harlot is Jezebel and destruction is her motive and she takes no prisoners. She is out to destroy anyone in her path. And she will always enter through the woman, thus the need for the man to be alert and in touch with the Father. He is her covering and partner to come into agreement and pray against these attacks. The husband is not to misunderstand that this gives him the right to become a dictator or demanding boss. He is to allow her to make choices just like God allows him. Some will fail and be wrong at times. He must then be able to restore and fix what has been broken, giving sound and reasonable counsel, not abusive language. Proverbs 15:1 says, "A gentle answer turns away wrath, but a harsh word stirs up anger."

The woman also has a big role in keeping Jezebel out of the family. She must realize that she is the avenue that Jezebel will use to enter. This is not said to be condescending, it is just the way that it has happened and will happen over the course of history. She needs to be understanding of the pressures on the man to be head over the household and work with him and not against him. She must be careful not to allow the modern assumptions of society to confuse her into thinking that she is equal in the family. She is the partner but he must be the head according to God's order.

The woman needs to return the compassion and understanding that the man should have toward her, allowing the fruits of the Spirit to work within her so that they may be carried on into the children. She must be submissive to her husband and he must not be contentious towards her or the children. When she is having a bad day she should seek his help and wisdom, and not be quick to take offense or argue but understand that there must be a decision and he will not be right all the time. He is only taking the symbolic place of God in the family; he is not God and will make mistakes.

She must not take her problems out into the public and air them. She is to speak them with self-control to her husband, not being given to the temptation of being verbally abusive or even physically abusive. And the wife and husband should never argue and allow Jezebel to divide them in the viewing of the children. That is abusive and must not be allowed. Any division between mother and father brings fear and instability to the children and causes them to rebel.

IN THE CHURCH

Rebellion is the reason that our society has been denigrated to the levels that we have fallen to. And we have the spirit of Jezebel to thank for most of it. She continues to try and overrule the order of God. The rebellion to God's order and the deception of Jezebel has led to the moral decay of society and the destruction of the family unit. This spirit has been allowed to move into the church and is a cause of the church becoming so religious, built on the traditions of men rather than the obedience to God's word.

The church, as has been stated, is made up of people and families and when the family is being divided and destroyed so will the church. And it is the church's duty to see that the families are well guided with the Word of God so as not to allow the plan of the enemy to divide and destroy the church.

Unfortunately in this generation, the religious spirit of Jezebel has infiltrated the church and not much is being done about it. This is a result of the church being lulled into a sense of security through many teachings of the false prophets and the ignorance to the real revelation of the Word.

The modern day church has an attitude that she is a "New Testament" church without need for the "Old Testament" or Law of Moses. The church, her pastors, priests, elders, and the heads of denominations, should reread Acts chapter 28 and they would find that the church's witness and testimony should be coming from the Prophets and the Law. Paul, at the end of chapter 28, is using these two to try and persuade the people that this Jesus that he was giving testimony to was and is the Christ of God. This is the model that the church was to use in becoming the body that would receive the return of

Jesus Christ to this earth. Instead she has played the harlot falling for the teaching of Balaam, running after the money and riches of the earth rather than hearing what the Spirit says and seeing the true riches of the Heavenly Word and proclaiming them to this generation.

In writing and reading this, we can then come to the conclusion for what the need for winning the victory over Jezebel is: the revelation of the Word brought to us by the Holy Spirit. It is this revelation that will bring a common sense seeing of the Word so that the families and the church will not have to continue in the darkness of deception and ignorance. Putting this to use will then pave the way for peace in the families and ultimately victory in the church.

First there is the need to understand how to read and see the Word. To do this you will need to understand a few basic principles of how the Word was written.

• Number one, and the hardest to comprehend, is that the Word of God doesn't change. God gave this Word in a way that human beings could understand it and it is written in its simplest format. The formats that will be discussed do not change and are usable throughout the Bible. Don't rebel and fight the Holy Spirit, but allow the order of God to work in your hearing and seeing. If you will, you can then be on your way to defeating Jezebel.

The first format that we will reveal is the "pattern and shadow" viewing of the Word. Everything that is perishable has to be transformed into something imperishable.

What was made earthly or fleshly must be changed into something that is heavenly or spiritual. The Bible uses many examples of this format, for instance the passage, "whatever is Mine is Thine and Thine is Mine." It also uses this principle in the changing of

people's names. Saul was then named Paul, Jacob to
Israel, Abram to Abraham, and Jesus to Jesus Christ.

The Bible gives this revelation in the book of Exodus
chapters 25:1-27:19 where the pattern for the
tabernacle was given to Moses. The symbolism of the
furniture and articles for the tabernacle represent the
way God works; a pattern must have a shadow. And
common sense will tell us that a shadow has the same
common point with the bottom of the pattern.

Your shadow is linked to your feet when you are
standing. Therefore in viewing these chapters in
Exodus we gain this insight into the Word: The Ark
represents God, the Table of Showbread Jesus (the
bread from heaven); the Lampstand represents the
Spirit of God. From there we than can "see" the
transformation with the common point.

The Curtains of Linen represent the Holy Spirit, the

coverings and supports Jesus Christ, and the Veil
the Father in the Holy of Holies.

The instructions were given to Moses in this distinct
order so that we may have the way God intended for
us to build the tabernacle within us through the
understanding and revelation of His Word. See
illustration number one:

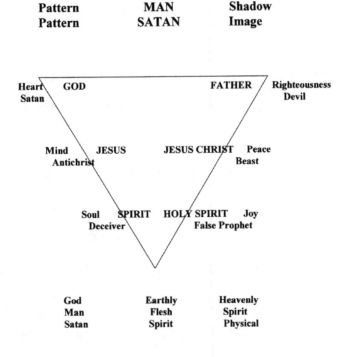

- The second format is the knowledge that the Lord is the Light in the darkness. In Genesis 1 the Bible says that God saw that the light was good and separated the light from the darkness calling the light day and the darkness night. He only called the light good, thus giving us a clue about future verses. When we can find the light being separated from the darkness we can then understand good from evil in the context that the Bible is being written in. Again in the book of Exodus we are given an example of what to look for. Chapters 10-12 show us that there was darkness in the land of Egypt as the next to last judgment.

The Bible then gives us the commandment of the Passover and the blood of the sacrificed lamb fulfilled by Jesus. We then are given the last plague that happened at midnight, or in the dark of night, of the striking down of the first born of Egypt. Jesus showed up in the middle of the darkness just like He does in your life and in the revealing of the written word.

A very important example of this in the Bible writings comes in understanding the three days that Jesus spent in the tomb.

The Bible tells us that there are twelve hours in a day. Therefore Jesus was crucified on a Friday, having the day darkened by God from noon till three to show Him as the light in the darkness. The Passover Lamb was laid in the tomb from Friday evening until Saturday morning (one day), on the Sabbath day or until Saturday evening (two days), from Saturday evening to Sunday morning (three days) and He was gone.

You will also notice that the light of the

Sabbath Day is in the middle of the darkness
in seeing the three days in the tomb. When
reading the Bible look to find this way of
writing and you will find Jesus and the ways of
the enemy revealed. Conversely, when you see
the darkness in between two lights you will
have the spirit of anti-christ and the beast
revealed. See illustration number two.

Jesus' 3 Days In The Tomb

| Friday Evening
To
Saturday Morning
(Preparation Day) | Saturday Morning
To
Saturday Evening
(Sabbath Day) | Saturday Evening
To
Sunday Morning
(1st Day of Week) |

~~~~~~

Spirit of Antichrist / Mark of The Beast

| **6 pm** | to | **6 am** | to | **6 pm** |

~~~~~~

Sign of Jonah

| Good | Bad | Good | Bad | Good | Bad |

| [3 Days] | & | [3 Nights] |

- The third format to reveal is the healing of the heart. The Bible tells us that the commandments will be written on tablets of stone and on the tablets of our heart.

The Ten Commandments were written in a way that the first five that were given were written on the left tablet as we view it and the second five written on the right. Understanding this, we can then see that the transgressions and iniquities that we are to repent of are those on the left and the sins that we are forgiven are written on the right.

It is a form of the "pattern and shadow" only it reveals the baptism of repentance that leads to the forgiveness of sins.

Don't allow the modern day religious teachings to deceive you. You must repent of the choices of old that you made and then be transformed into a new creation wherein the need for forgiveness of sins in the name of Jesus Christ can be granted to you by the grace of God the Father.

With this revelation, the attributes given to Satan and the devil are given to us to be able to pray and know who is attacking us. A word to the wise: don't think that certain words in the Bible can be exchanged with one another. Remember, His word doesn't change so don't you change it.

Satan will be used to describe the tempter of the commandments on the left tablet and the devil will be used to describe the tempter of the commandments on the right.

The devil is the physical manifestation of Satan and will try to resurrect your flesh against your spirit so that in getting you to live in the flesh Satan can then kill your soul.

Going back and forth from left to right and right to left will bring greater understanding of the Word and how each name and description of the separate entities in scripture are used to reveal good and evil. See illustration number three.

These are the formats that are so important to be able to understand and use the revelation of the words in the Bible for our victory as a church and for gaining everyday peace and joy in the families.

When the teachers of the Word learn to use these, we will see the religious ways of the spirit of Jezebel begin to be cast out of the church. Until then we will continue to see a church wrapped in tradition seeking the ways of Balaam.

Four Horns Of The Altar
JESUS CHRIST
Healed Our Broken Heart

MATTHEW
Law

No other gods

No idols

Don't take the Lord's name in vain

JOHN
Grace

Don't murder

Don't commit adultery

Don't steal

GOSPEL OF JESUS CHRIST

Keep Sabbath day holy   No false witness

Honor your   Don't covet
father   your
and   neighbor's
mother   things

EARTHLY

HEAVENLY

MARK
Mercy

LUKE
Healing

REPENTANCE
OF
LAWLESSNESS
We repent because
We haven't seen Messiah
(Transgressions/Iniquities)

FORGIVENESS
OF
SINS
The weakness of
our flesh

SCOURGING
for our
LAWLESSNESS

CRUCIFIXION
for our
SINS

EMPTY TOMB
victory over
DEATH

Balaam taught Balak how to speak to deceive the Israelites. He taught him to speak in Aramaic form instead of the Hebraic thus keeping the freeing revelation of the word from them. The same as the church is teaching using the "New Testament" and forgetting about the Law. Not understanding that the Law and the Prophets teach us of the Hebraic roots of our belief in Christ, the teaching and understanding that will reveal Jesus Christ to the rest of the world. The destructive forces of Satan in the form of Jezebel are at work again.

IN PROPHECY

Now that we have introduced you to these formats we can go forward using these to bring greater revelation to the workings and ways of Jezebel. When we expose Satan he must leave, according to scripture, because he hates the Light that reveals him. And in the days of this generation when we "see" the word being revealed in such a way we can then begin to understand the prophecies that pertain to the last days of the latter years. The days in which we will see the final prophecies fulfilled leading to the return of Jesus Christ and the captivity of Satan. In these days we will see that Jezebel and her spirit will manifest greatly as it did in the days of Elijah, the prophet whose spirit must come before the Lord can return. Using the knowledge that has been given to us, let us now understand and gain wisdom of these prophecies dealing with Jezebel.

The book of Revelation chapter 2 in the letter to the church at Thyatira tells us about some of the characteristics of Jezebel. We are able to use these to go back in scripture to allow the Bible to explain the prophecies that deal with Jezebel. The verses tell us that she takes aim at the Lord's bondservants by teaching them and leading them astray.

A bondservant is a person who loves the Lord enough to obey His commandments, statutes, and laws. He loves his wife and children enough so as not to leave them and not to allow Satan to rule in his household. He loves with an unconditional love like the Lord gives to him. And it is with that love that he will keep the order in his family and in the church no matter what the consequences. He will not allow Jezebel to divide and destroy. He trains himself with the Word of God to be able to discern and detect when she is trying to enter, to be able to know the way for victory. It is these bondservants that this book of Revelation was written to. These are the ones who are able to hear the Word and see the Word.

Jezebel attacks these bondservants just like she did Elijah and the prophets of old because these are the ones who have the wisdom to overcome her and expose her with the true Word of God, not a false theology.

It is with these false theologies that she attempts to lead the Lord's bondservants into immoral acts. These immoral acts are the transgressions and iniquities that have been repented of but, if not careful, the bondservant can be subjected to adulterous relations so as to be deceived into a fallen state. Look again at this illustration of the two tablets of the heart.

Adultery is one of the second sets of five commandments written on the right side of the heart. If Jezebel can tempt your flesh into an adulterous relationship she then leads you back into the left side of the heart where the immorality exists according to the Bible.

This is where Satan then can kill and destroy as he roams about on the earth. When this occurs repentance again is needed and prayer made for the "sick" person is needed from and with the elders. God then will heal and raise that person back up and forgive any sins that there are. He will be restored.

If the person fails to obey and repent, he will lay with Jezebel on this bed of sickness continuing in this sin of adultery with the harlot. The Bible says that great tribulation will be their reward for these deeds and the children will die of pestilence. This gives us the need for the husband to be the head of the house and the woman to work in partnership with him as has been written before. The Bible tells us that there will be a time of Great Tribulation coming that there has never been anything like it nor will there ever be anything like it again. It is this spirit we can then understand will be the main scheme of Satan as the Day of the Lord draws near.

As we continue in what the prophecies say about Jezebel, we must understand that the sign of her activities given to this generation, the evil and adulterous one, will be the sign of Jonah. Using the second format (see illustration number 2) in understanding scripture, we then can understand what this sign is and what Jonah did that has end time meaning. Jonah began as a prophet of God. He then made a bad decision by not obeying God and going to Nineveh telling them of their wickedness and their need for repentance. After being swallowed by the great fish he then repented and then called out to God for deliverance. Upon the Lord responding to his cries, he went to Nineveh and when the Lord received their cry of repentance he became angry towards the

Lord. Upon the Lord reasoning with him, he went out and he became happy for the blessing of the plant for shade the Lord had given him. But upon the Lord having the plant taken away, Jonah then chose death over life.

To put this into perspective using the second format, Jonah was good (light) then was bad (dark), was good, then bad, good, and then finished badly. Viewing this we have the three days and the three nights that Jesus spoke of when He gave the sign we would be given. The good being the days and the bad being the nights.

This is important in the understanding of many prophecies, to be able to know what the seal of the bondservants and what the mark of the beast is. The seal of the bondservants is the Holy Spirit and His mark is of a light surrounded by two dark entities. Whereas the mark of the beast in the spirit of the anti-christ is a dark surrounded by two entities of light.

We can then use what Jonah did and didn't do and the sign revealed therein to see why Jesus said the men of Nineveh would stand with this generation and condemn it because Nineveh repented at the warning of Jonah but the generation that lived in Jerusalem did not when the Savior Himself was there proclaiming repentance to them. Now comes some understanding and wisdom pertaining to prophecy.

In the book of Nahum chapter 3:4, the Bible reveals to us the Lord's viewpoint towards what was happening in the wickedness that was in Nineveh. There were many harlotries of the harlot, the charming one, the mistress of sorceries, who sells nations by her harlotries and families by her sorceries. This is proclaiming the same things of destruction that Jezebel is and has been creating under the power of Satan. Nineveh is stated as being the great city in

Jonah 1:2 and is made reference to in Revelation 17:18.

We also know that the title of "the great city" is given to other cities as we continue in the gathering of the knowledge of the prophecies. The prophecy of Zechariah chapter 5 sheds some more light on this as Zechariah is given an insight to a vision. He saw an ephah with a woman sitting inside with a lead covering and the angel said that this was Wickedness (Nineveh) in the middle and the lead weight was on its opening. The lead weight was very heavy in the same way that Jerusalem is described in Zechariah 12:3 as a heavy stone. It was a heavy stone that was rolled over the mouth of the tomb of Jesus in Jerusalem after He made the way for the repentance of our wickedness and was preparing the way for victory over death, the penalty for our sins.

Then we are shown by Zechariah, again in chapter 5, that this ephah with the woman inside was taken to the land of Shinar, (the meaning of the name of Shinar is "change of the city" which was where they undertook to build the Tower of Babel) or with some understanding Babylon. Thus the great city changed from being Nineveh to Jerusalem to Babylon, understanding that the city God chose to dwell in, Jerusalem, is in the middle surrounded by two cities of wickedness.

Having established this knowledge, understanding can be obtained from what John saw in Revelation 17 and 18. John saw Jezebel, the woman on the scarlet beast clothed with the garments of the King, the purple and scarlet, instead of the garments of the bride, the white linen. John saw Jezebel usurping the order of God just as she had done throughout the Bible. She is the Mother of all Harlots bringing with her the confusion of Babylon. She has in her hand a cup of the abominations and immoralities she has lead the bondservants into. The cup is also full of the blood of the saints and witnesses, the prophets Jezebel had killed.

After you have gained knowledge and that knowledge becomes understanding, then you may have the wisdom to know the rest of the prophecy.

The seven heads and the ten horns can be understood from 1Chronicles chapter 2. The seven kings come from the descendant of Judah, Zerah. Verse 6 states that the sons of Zerah were Zimri, Ethan, Heman, Calcol, and Dara; five in all. These are the five that have fallen. The one who is would be Achan, the troubler of Israel from the book of the prophecies of Joshua (Yeshua) who caused the defeat of the Israelites by taking things that were not to be taken. Idolatry would be the definition of this sin and the type of temptation that Jezebel teaches the Lord's

bondservants to indulge in. The seventh is listed as
the son of Ethan, whose name can mean wisdom, thus
the mind that has wisdom, or Azariah. The beast is an
eighth because he brings a strange fire as an
abomination before the Lord as did Nadab and Abihu
in the Torah lesson entitled "the Eighth" but he is one
of the seven or the one who is yet to come.

John saw the ten horns as being the sons of Israel
listed in the book of 1Chronicles chapter 2 also. He
pointed out ten as making up the horns of the beast
instead of twelve because the Levites were not
counted normally with the rest and they were God's
possession. The other tribe that would not be included
with the beast would be the tribe of Joseph.

The prophecy spoken to Joseph in Genesis 49 tells us
that the crown would be on his head distinguished
from his brothers. These ten have not yet received a

kingdom so the tribes of Joseph and Levi would not
be seen as horns of the beast.

It is these ten and the beast that hate the harlot
because she continues to usurp the order of authority.
But it is also these that eat her flesh as the dogs did
Jezebel's before her corpse was spread over the field
as dung. It is this dung or manure pile and field or soil
that the salt of the earth is useless for if it loses its
taste. It becomes good for nothing except to be
trampled under foot by men, just like Jezebel was
trampled under foot.

The Bible does give us the hope of the defeat of
Babylon and the setting free of those held captive
within her. This is the place where the nation of Judah
was taken into captivity. And Judah's legacy is much
like that of Jonah. Judah was sometimes good and
sometimes bad.

We then can see that the spirit of anti-christ, Judaism, comes from Judah and is revealed as we "see" the adulterous act that he did with Tamar playing the harlot. The act that produced the twins Perez, where the lineage of Jesus comes from, and Zerah, where we have just learned the beast comes from. It is the act that is written between two discussions of Joseph as he symbolizes Jesus in the Torah lesson from Genesis chapters 37 through 40.

Format number two is used here to bring understanding to the warning from the Lord that the light within us is not darkness, denying that Jesus is the Son of God by our lack of understanding and falling for the confusion (Babylon's meaning) brought by Jezebel with the power of the deceiver, Satan. Not falling for and selling out to the temptation of the teaching of Balaam within the religious system today, but using the knowledge, insight, and wisdom that the

Holy Spirit has shown us by the revelation of the Word.

We have used the Book of Revelation quite a bit in understanding prophecy and we should not omit the end time Book of Daniel. Daniel was the man that the Lord used to separate the Law of Moses into the 54 Torah lessons while in the captivity of Judah in Babylon.

It is with the revelation of the prophecies contained within these lessons that the Book of Daniel will also be understood because through these lessons Daniel was given his visions and wisdom to write. And as we "see" what Daniel had revealed to him, we can understand the main vision he saw was the deception, sorceries, and trouble the spirit of Jezebel would be causing for people at the end of time.

It will be the same Jezebel that gave Elijah trouble, the same spirit of Jezebel that manifested in Herodias to bring death to John the Baptist, the one who had the mantle of Elijah in those days, that will be causing trouble as the mantle of Elijah is again seen to prepare for the coming of the Lord as the prophecy states. And it is for the reason of Jezebel usurping the order of authority and the Lord's Revelation to his bondservants that the beast in Daniel chapter 11 will have no desire for woman. If he did, his kingdom could be divided, not being able to stand and being easily revealed.

DEALING WITH HER

We have gained much insight into what the Bible tells us about Jezebel and what she has been and will be doing to a greater degree in the great tribulation. The next need we have is to then understand what we can do to win the victory over her.

The first thing we must do is to understand that this time of the end is coming quickly upon us as we see Jezebel taking a more prominent role in our societies.

Some would rather hide their heads in the sand and pretend that it is just the way we are progressing as a human race and that there is nothing to be done about it. That is wrong and a very selfish attitude especially when we think about the world we are preparing for the children to grow up in. People should have the attitude when raising children not to just provide food, clothing, and shelter for them but to create and be a part of making the world and their community as good or better to grow up and live in as they had when they were children.

In defeating any enemy it is always an advantage to know the ways your enemy will operate in to try and defeat you. Satan, working as Jezebel, has several plans that the Bible gives us insight into. Understand this, though what will be written might seem easy to detect and understand, Jezebel is tricky and sneaky in her activities. Do not underestimate her as a foe.

Jezebel will have tendencies to be very repetitive in what she does and says. She can be very annoying and create situations to get you off your guard and lose the self-control that is so necessary in maintaining the victory over her. Just let someone continue to remind you of what you are doing wrong over and over and see how aggravated you become.

This is one way that causes many arguments in marriages and is a cause of abuse. Jezebel likes it when a husband and wife argue, especially in front of the children. You must not allow this to happen and lose this part of the confrontation with Jezebel.

One biblical example of this happens when Satan is allowed to put Job to the test. After Satan had killed his children and stolen from him his wealth, he was allowed to attack Job's flesh and physical health.

We can imagine that patience was decreasing and discouragement was increasing with Job and his wife by now. There was probably not a lot of joy and peace in this household and several unhappy discussions between Job and his wife were occurring.

While Job was dealing with the pains and humility of this, his wife finally came along, in the spirit of

Jezebel, and tested his spirit by telling him to curse God and die. Job's answer to her overcame Jezebel when he told her she was speaking as one of the foolish women speaks, asking her if they should accept the good from God and not accept adversity.

At first glance we could probably think that Job had just created an environment for an incredible argument but in the reality of it Job won the victory by seeing what was happening and taking authority over the situation, all the while not allowing sin to come from his lips and Jezebel's temptation to cause him to do something stupid to his wife.

He also sent the message into the spiritual realm that he was not going to allow this to manifest into something greater. He was not going to allow Jezebel to make a mountain out of a molehill. With his faith and belief he moved the mountain and cast it into the sea to be cleansed from this iniquity. We can see how this happens and can be applied to the family situation in today's world.

The Jezebel spirit uses the temptation of adultery to divide and conquer. This can happen very subtly and in the immoral and sexually permissive society we have become is not looked upon as the travesty and the sin it is. This has become an acceptable way of life because Jezebel has not been revealed and taken control of while the end times events as prophecy says will unfold take place.

Adultery can be described in two ways pertaining to Jezebel and to what the biblical understanding says. The first way is the most common and what you would think if first, the sexual impropriety between a man and woman where one or both is married to another. There isn't much that needs to be said about this except the need to recognize it as a devilish/Satanic attack that will lead to the lust of the flesh.

There are various reasons that create the avenue for Jezebel to sneak into people's lives in this aspect and one must be alert and overcome this temptation or the destruction of the family is evident, most often ending in divorce and great pain to all the parties involved.

The second way to describe adultery is in a spiritual context and is more difficult to discern and is most often the most destructive. The Lord hates divorce, not just between men and women, but also towards His Son, the bridegroom. Jesus tells us the only reason for divorce is unchastity and whoever divorces his wife for any other reason makes her to commit adultery and whoever marries a divorced woman commits adultery.

He is telling us if any wife will not let her husband be the head and she will not realize and allow him to overcome the spirit of Jezebel attacking her that she has become unchaste, committing adultery by clinging to and not allowing herself to be set free from this spirit.

She likes the situation that Jezebel is creating for her rather than what God has planned for her within the family. The Bible explains it is for this reason of disobedience that a divorce is allowed by God but yet He hates it because Satan has been allowed a small victory in the lives of His children.

The meaning of not allowing a man to marry a divorced woman without sin can then be understood. He should recognize that she has embraced Jezebel and if he were to marry her he would become one flesh with her, tempting himself to become unchaste in his relationship with God thus creating another family unit out of order.

As we can see from Job's example, his wife must have listened and allowed Job to do what he knew to be right because we do not read of a divorce happening between the two, only a double blessing from the Lord as they overcame Satan's test.

This doesn't conclude there is no hope for the woman. There are ways of deliverance from this spirit that will take elders with knowledge to anoint and pray for her deliverance from the "sickness" of this spirit.

God will heal her and raise her up forgiving any sin she has committed, renewing her to wholeness and cleanliness in Jesus Christ. She is then capable of remarrying, being blessed with the grace of God.

These are the major two ways that Jezebel is stealing, killing, and destroying the family unit and the church. There are others that need to be watched for.

- She will try to bring great confusion in many circumstances, arguing about things that she knows nothing about.
- She brings impurity not only to the Word of God, but lies and distorts the truth in many circumstances.
- She will bring misunderstanding to what is good and evil, what is obedience to God and what is tradition to men.
- Jezebel will try and justify her deceptive ways and lure families and the church into following her sin and transgression.

In our society she is being accepted in her works of divination, the explosion of the use of psychics and fortune telling devices. The reading of horoscopes and people seeking what the future holds in store from dark sources.

The tattooing and body piercing that is so widely being done is a work of Satan and Jezebel against God's commands and is not being recognized as such.

She is enticing men in her seductive ways to wear goatees and haircuts that produce the look of evil and are against the Word of God. We are to have a look of godliness, not wearing symbols of evilness.

The increase in child pornography has led to an increase in sexual immorality in the society and is another working of this spirit because the men are falling into it and not taking authority to stop it, being accepted and being tempted by it.

The respect for the elders of the world and their welfare, the disrespect of children to parents, the lack

of love amongst people, and the increase of
dishonest ways of business are all a result and are
accredited to in the Bible to Satan working in the form
of Jezebel.

Soon it becomes quite evident that the many problems
in our families, church and the world are the result of
this type of spiritual activity. And it is with this
knowledge we can see that we are getting closer to the
end times as the activity increases. And as it increases
our knowledge and understanding will increase to
defeat it if we will allow it.

This victory would seem to be an impossible task in
our eyes as we see it overwhelming society today. But
it is with this impossible realization we then can
surrender and come to know we must learn the way to
victory from our Almighty God.

We have seen how Job secured his victory by recognizing it and standing his ground against the temptation. Jesus overcame it by knowing what was written and how it was written in the scriptures, then speaking correctly the Word to expose and deliver others from the deceptive acts.

 Paul recognized the annoyance and claimed the victory by casting it out of the girl with a spirit of divination with these few words, "I command you in the name of Jesus Christ to come out of her!"

Jesus also gave us an answer for overcoming it in our families when He answered the crowd saying His mother, sisters, and brothers were those who do the will of His Father in heaven. He had nothing to do with those that continue to embrace and not reject the ways of Jezebel. Even with His mother at the marriage supper at Cana when she began to give Him orders in what to do about the wine being gone. She wanted Him to create a miracle by her orders and in her time frame and He quietly answered her by saying "what do I have to do with you, woman?" He was speaking not to His mother Mary but the spirit of Jezebel that was trying to usurp His and His Father's positions.

The Bible teaches us by these and other examples that the victory over Jezebel comes from gaining the wisdom of the true Word of God and not man's theological traditions.

It is those that have aided in our ignorance to the schemes of Jezebel in this time and by the mercy and grace of God, He is now giving us the insight to victory over her. This victory, as we have seen, doesn't have to come with fights and arguments, but with the self-control we have if we stay in the ways of the Holy Spirit.

The victory will come quicker with words of firmness, but with compassion, as we see the person being tormented rather than the person as the enemy. The Bible tells us "a gentle answer turns away wrath but a harsh word stirs up anger." Jezebel will try and get you frustrated, discouraged, angry, and vengeful if you allow her.

Keep your cool and defeat Jezebel, don't beat yourself, your spouse, or your children by being physically or mentally abusive.

CONCLUSION

We have covered many aspects of Jezebel and several
biblical applications to understand the spiritual
warfare that we are in the midst of. Of course there
are others that could be written about, but then again
they already have been in a Book called the Bible.

With God's blessing and grace hopefully there has
been a revelation of His Word shown in this transcript
that can be used to increase your knowledge of the
Bible to use it as the life book God meant it to be.

I can tell you it is Jezebel who creates much of the
depressions in people's lives today. These depressions
cause great abuse both mentally and physically in the
lives of many. The causes of the depressions can vary
but many are caused in the family by money issues, a
huge and often used avenue for Jezebel.

Whether it is the lack of money or the abundance of it, she will use money to be a root to grow her evil deeds from. They are treated with therapy and drugs but also need to be prayed against, seeking the healing of heaven in these cases.

I have seen men just give up and patronize situations like these instead of using their God given abilities to overcome them. Men need to be paying more attention to their relationship with God today and a little less about the other cares of life. The cares of life will begin to get taken care of if they would just build their relationships with God and declare that their households will serve the Lord.

The Satanic works of Jezebel do not take prisoners. He is out to kill steal and destroy as he roams about on the earth. When you are in war, prisoners are taken alive, not dead. It has often been said that you will live somewhere forever, in heaven or in hell. The fact is only in heaven will you live. In hell you will be dead yet still being tormented by Jezebel as she reminds you of how she tricked you and made you fall into her deceptive ways, eventually denying Christ by putting Satan in His place.

Remember the anger and aggravation that the repetitive ways of Jezebel tempt you with. In hell these will be a constant occurrence with weeping and gnashing of teeth by those who are judged to hell for all eternity.

No one has done anything to you to deserve this; they have only rebelled against God. We should have enough compassion for others to prepare ourselves to help them keep from this eternal damnation. Sometimes, unfortunately, we have to turn their flesh back over to Satan so that in the end maybe their soul can be saved.

To encourage you to get prepared I would remind you that you will gain personal satisfaction in seeing other individuals and families set free from the pains of Jezebel's activities. You will also be preparing yourself to be called a bondservant of God, taking part in the first resurrection to rule and reign with Christ.

Being a bondservant of God should be the goal of all the believers of Jesus Christ. A bondservant loves his Master, his wife, and his children and chooses to serve His Master all the days of his life. He will come under the attack of Jezebel more than someone else but the Father will not allow her to destroy or kill him. He will have the mysteries and prophecies of the Bible revealed to him like the prophets of old, beginning with the understanding of our Hebraic roots in the Law of Moses. This is the reason Jezebel comes after him more than others, she tries to kill the prophets who can identify and reveal her.

I have seen in my life the spirit of Jezebel destroy individual lives and families. Personally, I have thought of this years ago and decided it would be the one thing that if given one wish to rid the world of whatever I wanted, this would be my choice.

I didn't realize it at the time what name to put on this request, but after the revelation from the Holy Word, I thankfully know and understand what to call "it". And yet with this understanding comes some sadness and yet joy.

Sadness because I realize, unlike the possibility of other problems in the world being done away with, this problem will not go away until the return of our Lord, Jesus Christ. It will be with us until that day and even for a short time after when Satan is released from captivity.

Joy because God has granted us all, with the revealing of the ways of this "sickness," the way to be victorious over it and bring healing to individuals, families, and the church.

As Satan continues to roam about the earth we must take this Gospel message to the ends of the earth to defeat Him. My prayer is whoever reads or hears this revelation will become convicted by the Holy Spirit to commit their lives and families to overcome Jezebel and her temptations. And those who believe will join in the quest to bring deliverance and victory to others over her with the wisdom, knowledge, and understanding of the complete Gospel of Jesus Christ

Printed in the United States
By Bookmasters